Original title:
Winter's Symphony

Copyright © 2024 Swan Charm
All rights reserved.

Author: Aron Pilviste
ISBN HARDBACK: 978-9916-79-477-7
ISBN PAPERBACK: 978-9916-79-478-4
ISBN EBOOK: 978-9916-79-479-1

Silent Sonata of the Blizzards

Whispers swirl in the frosty air,
Snowflakes dance without a care.
Each breath sharp, crisp as a knife,
Winter's chill brings stillness to life.

Branches bow under the weight,
Nature wraps in her white-skirt fate.
Silent echoes of the night's embrace,
A symphony's soft, serene grace.

Footprints linger, then fade away,
In the canvas of night, shadows play.
Moonlight glistens on silent streams,
Before the dawn breaks our lovely dreams.

Frosted whispers caress the ground,
In this stillness, peace is found.
Hearts wrapped warm in winter's cloth,
We hush our voices, hold our troth.

Underneath a starry dome,
We find tranquility, a quiet home.
Blizzards sing their rugged song,
In their arms, we feel we belong.

Frosted Harmonies

A sheet of white, pure and bright,
Frosted morning greets the light.
Each flake falls with gentle grace,
Painting joy upon the space.

Trees wear coats of shimmering lace,
Nature dons a wintry face.
The world wrapped in a glistening hug,
Promising warmth, a sweet snug drug.

Softly hums the winter breeze,
Whispers carry through frozen trees.
In the quiet, music flows,
Through the white where the cold wind blows.

Echoes of laughter, a child's delight,
Sleds glide fast, a joyful flight.
The air vibrates with pure delight,
As day melts slowly into night.

Under stars, skies drape so deep,
In the hush, the universe keeps.
Frosted harmonies fill the air,
In winter's song, we find our care.

Solitude in Snow

Gentle flakes drift down,
A blanket soft and white.
Whispers fill the silence,
As day gives way to night.

Footprints lost in white,
Echoes of a past roam.
In this wintry wonder,
I find a quiet home.

Branches wear their crystals,
Draped in nature's lace.
Time seems to surrender,
In this frozen space.

The world slows its heartbeat,
Underneath a pale glow.
In this hush of winter,
I learn to just let go.

Solitude surrounds me,
Wrapped in flurries' peace.
With each breath of the cold,
I find my heart's release.

Whispering Pines in Slumber

Beneath the moonlit sky,
The pines stand tall and proud.
In their peaceful shadows,
Silence speaks aloud.

Branches sway with dreams,
In cool night's tender breath.
Nature holds her secrets,
In the stillness of death.

Stars twinkle above,
A soft and twinkling sheen.
Every whispering breeze,
Carries tales unseen.

Resting under starlight,
The world begins to fade.
In this sacred moment,
New memories are made.

Wrapped in night's embrace,
The pines hold time at bay.
In their soft slumbering,
I yearn to fade away.

Frosty Interludes

In the morning's first light,
Frost clings to the ground.
Each blade glistens gently,
In beauty, we are bound.

Windows frost the colors,
Of a world dressed in white.
Nature's crystal canvas,
Glows in soft morning light.

Breath visible like ghosts,
On this chilly delight.
Every step feels gentle,
In the calm of the night.

A hush wraps around me,
As I step in the scene.
Frosty interludes dance,
In a world so serene.

Moments captured softly,
In a winter's embrace.
Time drifts like the flakes,
In the stillness of space.

The Color of Gray Skies

Overhead, clouds gather,
A blanket of deep gray.
Whispers of the coming rain,
Will chase the sun away.

In the somber stillness,
The world feels close at hand.
With every muted moment,
New thoughts begin to stand.

Shadows stretch and mingle,
As daylight starts to fade.
In this palette of gray,
The heart finds solace made.

Birds take flight in silence,
Through the misty expanse.
In the color of gray skies,
Life slows down to dance.

Echoes of the raindrops,
Whispering on the ground.
In the hue of gray skies,
A quiet peace is found.

Reflections in the Frost

Morning whispers soft and clear,
A world transformed, the chill draws near.
Glistening patterns in purest white,
Nature's canvas, a wondrous sight.

Footsteps print on fragile glass,
Each step a memory, moments pass.
Into the quiet, the heart takes flight,
In frozen stillness, the soul ignites.

Sunrise dances on icy streams,
Frosted edges, like silver dreams.
A gentle sigh from the earth's embrace,
Reflection captured, time's tender grace.

Whispers of winter, soft and sweet,
Silent magic beneath our feet.
In every flake and glimmering sheen,
Lies a story, a moment unseen.

As daylight fades, the stars emerge,
Frosty breath in the evening surge.
Through winter's veil, peace softly calls,
In the night's embrace, the silence falls.

The Chill's Resonance

Beneath the sky of leaden gray,
The chill wraps close, a soft ballet.
Each breath a cloud, a fleeting ghost,
In winter's grip, we gather most.

Branches creak with whispered fears,
Echoes carried through the years.
The air is sharp, the world stands still,
An icy calm, a quiet thrill.

Stars blink through a frosty shroud,
A gemstone night, both fierce and proud.
In this embrace of cold despair,
Hope lingers still, a whispered prayer.

Footsteps echo on frozen ground,
In the chill where dreams abound.
The heartbeats sync with nature's tune,
In harmony beneath the moon.

As shadows lengthen, the night descends,
The chill's embrace, where silence mends.
In every draft, in every sigh,
Lies the essence of winter's cry.

Celestial Haze

Veils of mist wrap the horizon,
Stars peek through, a silent season.
The moon's glow spills on frosty leaves,
In twilight's hush, the heart believes.

Whispers of night on the cool breeze,
A dance of shadows among the trees.
Celestial light, a shimmering haze,
Guides the wanderer through the maze.

Each step is soft, a gentle glide,
In this soft light, the dreams reside.
Awash in wonder, lost in time,
Nature drapes us in calming rhyme.

As the world sleeps under a starry dome,
The heart finds peace, the mind finds home.
In the stillness, a voice calls clear,
Echoing love from far and near.

Dawn's embrace will soon unfold,
But for now, we cradle the cold.
In this celestial, fleeting phase,
We find our truth in the night's gaze.

Enigmatic Ice

Fractured patterns of light and shade,
Holding secrets in every blade.
A crystalline world, so fiercely bright,
Whispers of wonder in the night.

Lakes mirror thoughts, both deep and vast,
Ancient stories in silence cast.
In the chill, there's warmth to find,
As ice and soul weave, intertwined.

Footprints lead where few have tread,
Paths of frost, where dreams are bred.
Nature's riddle beneath the skin,
In the quiet, let the journey begin.

Misty echoes and resonate sighs,
Each shard of ice, a truth belies.
Hidden depths in every glance,
The dance of winter, a mystic trance.

As twilight falls, the stars take flight,
Revealing wonders in the night.
In the enigmatic, we seek release,
In frozen realms, we find our peace.

Chilling Muse

In the stillness of the night,
Whispers dance, inviting dreams,
Fingers trace the frosty air,
A muse in silence softly gleams.

Stars above begin to glow,
Casting light on shadowed ground,
Footsteps leave a fleeting mark,
In this world, my heart is found.

Echoes of the winter's breath,
Whirl and twirl like snowflakes' flight,
Every heartbeat feels the chill,
Wrapped in warmth, I bask in light.

Time unwinds like threads of white,
Spinning tales of love and loss,
In the grasp of winter's hold,
Wisdom drapes like snow across.

With the dawn, the muse retreats,
Leaving trails of whispered thoughts,
In the heart, she sparks a flame,
Of creativity, dearly sought.

Snowdrift Melodies

Beneath a quilt of purest snow,
Nature sings in hushed refrain,
Each flake a note upon the ground,
A symphony of winter's reign.

Branches bow with crystal crowns,
The world a canvas, white and bright,
Whispers echo through the trees,
As day fades into the night.

In the distance, laughter rings,
Children play in soft embrace,
Footprints leading to the sky,
Joy resides in winter's grace.

As twilight casts its glittered charm,
The moon rises, a silver spoon,
Sipping scenes of frozen bliss,
Melodies beneath the moon.

Snowdrifts cradle hearts anew,
Each note a treasure to behold,
With every breath, the magic flows,
A story in the snow unfolds.

Ghosts of the Glaciers

In shadows deep, the whispers call,
Ghosts drift through the icy night,
Memories of a frozen past,
Like echoes flickering in flight.

Windswept tales of silent years,
Tell of journeys far and wide,
Glaciers sing their ancient songs,
Guardians of the world's pride.

Beneath the surface, secrets gleam,
Frozen tears of time's embrace,
Silent witnesses of change,
In this cold, they find their place.

With every thaw, the stories breathe,
Revealing truths once held too tight,
Nature's canvas shifts and sways,
As ghosts emerge from endless night.

Embrace the chill, and listen close,
To the wisdom the glaciers share,
For in their depths, we must believe,
Lie the echoes of our care.

Lanterns in the Snow

Huddled close in winter's clutch,
Lanterns glow in soft embrace,
Each flicker tells a story sweet,
Warming hearts in this cold space.

Drifting snowflakes kiss the ground,
While shadows dance on walls of white,
A tapestry of dreams unfurls,
Beneath the stars that shine so bright.

Voices float on frosty air,
Laughter mingles with the light,
In the stillness, time stands still,
As lantern's glow ignites the night.

Through the drifts, we wander forth,
Guided by the tender flame,
Every step an act of love,
In this magic, we're the same.

So hold the lanterns close to you,
Let their warmth dissolve your fears,
For in the snow, we find the spark,
That lights the way through all our years.

The Artistry of Ice

In the silence of winter's grace,
Frozen patterns softly trace.
Each crystal unique and bright,
A delicate dance in the pale moonlight.

Nature's canvas, pure and wide,
A masterpiece, time cannot hide.
Frosting branches, a twinkling glow,
Whispers of magic in the frosty snow.

Beneath the starlit, frosty skies,
Beauty captures wandering eyes.
Icy artworks, tranquil and free,
A fleeting glimpse of eternity.

Textures merge in sparkling hue,
Painting worlds where dreams come true.
Frozen rivers, paths unseen,
Reveal the artistry serene.

In the chill, the heart feels warm,
Nature's wonders, softly swarm.
As we marvel at the sight,
The artistry of ice ignites the night.

Hushed Flakes Falling

Gently from the heavens, they drift,
Snowflakes dance, a tender gift.
Silent whispers in the air,
A wintry magic beyond compare.

Each flake unique, a fleeting kiss,
Moments wrapped in winter's bliss.
Lying softly on the ground,
A quiet beauty all around.

As twilight falls, the world turns white,
Softly glimmering, a peaceful sight.
Under moon's embrace so bright,
Hushed flakes falling, pure delight.

Wrapped in warmth, we gaze outside,
Nature's wonder, our hearts abide.
With every flake that finds its place,
Hushed dreams come alive in grace.

Nocturne of the Cold

Under the blanket of the night,
Winter's breath, both sharp and light.
A symphony of chilling sounds,
In the darkness, beauty bounds.

Crickets hush, their songs are gone,
As frosty air starts to yawn.
Stars above begin to gleam,
Reflecting on the icy stream.

Moonlight spills on snow-kissed ground,
Whispers echo all around.
A nocturne softly starts to play,
Melodies of winter's sway.

Every shadow tells a tale,
In this stillness, hearts set sail.
Chasing dreams beneath the fold,
In the chilly night's stronghold.

As dawn approaches, colors blend,
This tranquil night, we won't pretend.
In the silence of the cold,
Life's soft secrets, we behold.

Glistening Dreams

In the dawn, a shimmer glows,
Reflecting on the winter snows.
Glistening dreams come to fruition,
In the heart, a warm ignition.

Sparkling light on every pane,
A world transformed, pure and plain.
Follow the path where shadows fade,
Glistening dreams in the frosty shade.

Crisp air carries whispers sweet,
With every breath, our hearts repeat.
The joy of simple, quiet things,
In glistening dreams, the spirit sings.

Underneath the azure sky,
Hope and wonder draw us nigh.
Like twinkling stars, we find our way,
In these glistening dreams, we play.

As winter's grace begins to wane,
Memories etched, like whispers strain.
In every corner, glimmers entice,
Embracing life, the art of ice.

Shimmering in Stillness

In twilight's grace, the water gleams,
Stars reflect like scattered dreams.
Silence whispers, softly speaks,
Time stands still, and stillness leaks.

Gentle waves kiss the shore,
Nature breathes, longing for more.
Moonlight dances on the lake,
Heartbeats pause, a breath to take.

Costumed trees in shades of gold,
Stories of the night unfold.
Shadowed paths invite a stroll,
In this quiet, find your soul.

Crickets chirp a lullaby,
Underneath the velvet sky.
Every twinkle, every sigh,
Seeks the depths where dreams may lie.

In stillness, secrets softly play,
Echoes of the fading day.
With every star, a wish is cast,
Embracing moments that won't last.

Echoes Beneath the Surface

Ripples spread on water's skin,
Whispers from where dreams begin.
Beneath the calm, a hidden sound,
Where past and present can be found.

A world unseen, where shadows glide,
Secrets flow with the turning tide.
Bubbles rise from depths unknown,
Each a story, each a tone.

Silvery fish darting past,
Holding memories, shadows cast.
In depths so deep, time drifts away,
Echoes of night, sounds of day.

A dance of currents, life in sway,
Living stories, come what may.
Treasure hunts in briny deep,
Finding visions, yours to keep.

Oceans roar with might and grace,
Yet within, a softer space.
Guardians dwell in watery gloom,
Creating beauty, life to bloom.

Choreography of the Cold

Frosted air, the world in white,
Crystalline flakes drift down at night.
In silence, winter takes its stage,
Nature's dance, a frozen page.

Footprints trace a fleeting line,
Wanderers in the chill, divine.
Trees adorned in icy lace,
Each branch holding winter's grace.

As daylight fades, the light enchants,
Moonbeams call, and shadows dance.
A ballet of the frigid breeze,
Swirling flakes that hide with ease.

Crystal ponds reflect the sky,
Where whispered secrets still lie.
A frosty sigh, a gentle breeze,
Nature's melody with ease.

In blushing dawn, warmth shall break,
The choreography we shall make.
In cold's embrace, we'll find our way,
For even winter holds a sway.

Storybook in White

Pages turn in crisp, white sheets,
Where snowflakes fall, each moment greets.
A tale unfolds in muted hues,
Every drift, a chapter to choose.

Beneath the cloak of winter's breath,
Lies a landscape kissed by death.
Yet from this chill, life brews anew,
In every flake, a story true.

Pine branches wear a frosted crown,
Whispers of dreams drift gently down.
A quiet quest, a winding trail,
In the hush, hearts unveil.

Children's laughter fills the air,
Snowmen stand, a joyful pair.
Each playful throw, a moment bright,
Crafting memories in purest white.

Underneath this quilted sky,
Imagination learns to fly.
In winter's book, we've found our part,
Writing tales with every heart.

Snowy Stanzas

Softly falls the snow, a quilt,
Nature's calm, its peace is built.
Whispers dance through frosty air,
In stillness, dreams begin to flare.

Blankets cover all we see,
A world transformed, serene and free.
Footsteps mark the crisp, white ground,
In winter's grasp, a joy is found.

Pines don white, a grand display,
Guiding hearts through the cold day.
Sunlight glints on frosty trees,
Creating magic with the breeze.

Children laugh, their voices bright,
Building snowmen, pure delight.
Snowflakes twirl in playful flight,
Evening glows with stars at night.

As the season turns its page,
Nature wraps us in its cage.
Each flake, a note in winter's song,
In snowy stanzas, we belong.

Tapestry of the Frosted Night

In the hush of frosty nights,
Moonlight casts its silver sights.
Wrapped in warmth, we gaze above,
Stars adorn the sky we love.

Whispers of the wind ensue,
Carrying the tales so true.
Each breath taken, a crystal sigh,
Painting dreams where wishes fly.

Sprinkled frost on window panes,
Nature's art, no need for frames.
Patterns weave in intricate lace,
A tapestry we can embrace.

Candles flicker, shadows sway,
In this chill, our hearts convey.
Hot cocoa warms our frozen hands,
As we trace our future plans.

Glistening snow in soft moonlight,
Endless beauty, pure delight.
In this night, peace grows and spreads,
In our dreams, where magic treads.

Hibernal Harmonies

Echoes linger in the cold,
Nature's secrets to unfold.
Crystalline notes fill the air,
In quietude, we find our care.

Underneath the snowy dome,
Every creature finds a home.
Silent nights weave tales of old,
In winter's grip, the heart is bold.

Branches sway with gentle grace,
A symphony in nature's space.
As frost kisses the sleeping land,
Harmony in winter's hand.

Days grow short, yet lights still gleam,
In the darkness, hope will beam.
Together, we embrace the chill,
With hibernal dreams to fulfill.

Hearts entwined in warmth we share,
Building memories, unaware.
In each note of winter's song,
Hibernal harmonies belong.

Unwritten Sonatas on Ice

Beneath the stars, the moonlight glows,
A canvas fresh where quiet flows.
Upon the ice, our spirits twine,
In unwritten sonatas, we align.

Skaters glide like whispers soft,
With every turn, they dream aloft.
Music plays in subtle lines,
Crafting tales in frosty vines.

Shadows dance on frozen streams,
Laced with echoes of our dreams.
The world around in silence speaks,
In winter's voice, our heart it seeks.

Every crackle, every glide,
With every breath, winter's pride.
Notes unfurl like lace in flight,
A masterpiece, pure as the night.

Here we linger, in white's embrace,
Each moment caught in nature's grace.
In unwritten sonatas, we find,
The rhythm of the heart and mind.

Twilight Frost

In the hush of winter's light,
Stars begin their quiet flight.
Whispers dance on icy sighs,
As twilight paints the evening skies.

Shadows stretch across the ground,
Nature's beauty all around.
Frosty breath in silver streams,
Casts a spell of fleeting dreams.

The nightingale's soft refrain,
Echoes through the frosty lane.
Each note wrapped in crystal air,
A serenade beyond compare.

Moonbeams slide on frozen tops,
Through the trees, the silence drops.
In the stillness, hearts entwine,
Underneath the starlit shrine.

With every sparkle, shadows blend,
In twilight's glow, we find a friend.
Holding tight to moments lost,
In the whispering frost we trust.

The Quietude of Snowfall

Snowflakes drift, a silent choir,
Blanketing the earth in white.
Each flake tells a tale so rare,
Whirling softly through the air.

Underneath the heavy skies,
Time stands still, the world complies.
Footprints vanish, secrets hide,
In the quiet, dreams abide.

Branches bow with gentle grace,
Nature's cloak, a soft embrace.
Every sound muffled near,
In this peace, we draw near.

Windswept whispers fill the night,
As stars twinkle, cold and bright.
Wrapped in blankets, hearts align,
In the snowfall's sweet design.

Evening deepens, shadows blend,
In this calm, all roads descend.
Harmony in white's embrace,
The stillness finds a sacred place.

Melancholy of the Bare Branches

Winter's breath, a chilling ghost,
Clings to trees that stand like hosts.
Bare branches reach to claim the sky,
In silence, answering the sigh.

Haunting echoes of what was green,
Mingle with the frost's shy sheen.
Twilight casts a softer hue,
Draped in memories, cold and true.

Every shadow tells a tale,
Of summer's laughter, bright and pale.
Where once blooms danced in the breeze,
Now only whispers haunt the trees.

Yet in this sorrow, beauty gleams,
Nature weaves through fraying seams.
In stillness, find the strength to face,
Melancholy's gentle grace.

As the moonlight bathes the land,
We learn to let go, understand.
In bare branches, hearts can feel,
A hopeful promise beneath the steel.

Sweet Nothings in the Cold

In the chill of winter's breath,
Warmth of words can conquer death.
Softly spoken, sweetly shared,
Moments cherished, love declared.

Frosted windows, laughter spills,
Heartbeats echo through the chills.
Hand in hand, we brave the night,
In the shadows, hearts ignite.

Whispers dance, like drifting snow,
Gentle thoughts that ebb and flow.
In this embrace, the world grows small,
As we find our joy through it all.

Every sigh, a promise made,
In winter's grasp, fears start to fade.
Sweet nothings, like a song,
Carry us where we belong.

As stars twinkle in the cold,
With each moment, stories unfold.
Together, in this quiet scene,
We find solace, soft and serene.

Serenade of the Silent Pines

Whispers weave through mighty trees,
A soft embrace, a gentle breeze.
Beneath the boughs, the shadows play,
As twilight fades to night from day.

Stars blink softly, sharing light,
While crickets serenade the night.
The moonlight dances on the ground,
In this haven, peace is found.

Branches sway, a lullaby,
Swaying dreams beneath the sky.
Each breath taken, fresh and pure,
In nature's arms, we find our cure.

Silent pines, your watchful eyes,
Guard our thoughts as time flies by.
In your presence, hearts align,
Forever bound, a love divine.

Chords Beneath the Ice

A frozen lake, a whispered tune,
Echoes soft beneath the moon.
Crystals sparkling, pure and bright,
Chords of winter, pure delight.

In the silence, music waits,
Each note dances, opening gates.
Underneath this icy shield,
Hidden treasures are revealed.

Melodies of the season's breath,
Woven songs that cheat at death.
Nature's heart in quiet strife,
Playing chords that bring us life.

Through the chill, the warmth will rise,
In simple notes, the spirit flies.
With every swell, with every sigh,
The chords beneath the ice reply.

Celestial Frost

In the dawn, a glimmering frost,
Nature's brush, no beauty lost.
Each blade of grass, a diamond fair,
Adorned beneath the silent air.

Softly whispers the chilly breeze,
Tender kisses on the trees.
A world awake, in silver light,
Celestial wonders, pure delight.

Footprints trace the snowy ground,
In this realm, calmness is found.
Where the heavens seem to pour,
Frosty gifts from the celestial shore.

With every flake, a story spun,
Of winter's grip, yet warmth is won.
For each cold snap, in time will fade,
Celestial frost, a masquerade.

Tremors in a Snowbound Dream

In silence deep, the world does sleep,
A tender peace, secrets we keep.
Beneath the snow, the earth does sigh,
Whispers soft, as time slips by.

But tremors stir in dreams of white,
Awakening the heart's delight.
Snowflakes swirling, wild and free,
Painting visions avidly.

Through frosted panes, the shadows creep,
In slumber's hold, the world is deep.
Yet hidden hopes begin to glow,
As warm hearts pulse beneath the snow.

The winter's grip cannot restrain,
The vibrant pulse of life's refrain.
Every tremor tells a tale,
Of dreams that dance, of hopes that sail.

The Quiet Canvas

A brush of dusk upon the hill,
Gentle strokes that time instills.
Whispers paint the fading light,
Colors blend into the night.

In shadows deep, the dreams unfold,
Stories whispered, soft and bold.
Each hue a tale, each shade a sigh,
On this canvas, nights pass by.

Stars emerge, like thoughts untold,
Silver threads through darkness rolled.
The moon, a lantern in the gloom,
Guides the heart to find its room.

Beneath the sky, the world sleeps tight,
Wrapped in the cloak of tranquil night.
The quiet canvas stretches wide,
Holding secrets time can't hide.

In this stillness, life takes flight,
Beauty blooms in silent light.
Eternal echo, soft embrace,
On this canvas, I find my place.

Echoes of Hibernation

Beneath the snow, the earth lies still,
Dreaming quiet, beneath the chill.
Whispers of life in slumber deep,
Nature's secrets softly keep.

Frosted branches, time stands still,
Silent woods, a tranquil thrill.
Echoes dance in winter's breath,
A gentle pause before the death.

Beneath the frost, the seeds awaken,
In silence, promises are taken.
The heart of spring waits patiently,
For warmth to wake its symphony.

Icicles hang like frozen dreams,
Caught in time's unyielding schemes.
A world asleep, yet full of light,
Echoes of life in quiet night.

As seasons shift and shadows fade,
Life emerges, unafraid.
Hibernation whispers soft and low,
In reverie, life starts to grow.

A Ballet of Snowdrifts

Softly falling, flake by flake,
The world transforms, a dance to wake.
Snowdrifts gather, gentle sway,
A ballet in the light of day.

Twirling whispers in the breeze,
Nature's art, a perfect tease.
Each drift a stage, each flake a star,
In winter's grasp, we wander far.

Children laugh, their spirits bright,
Building dreams in purest white.
Snowmen rise with joyful cheer,
As winter's rhythm draws them near.

Footprints trace a winding tale,
In the silence, soft and pale.
A fleeting dance, a moment's grace,
The ballet of the snowflakes' embrace.

As twilight falls and shadows grow,
Whispers pulse beneath the snow.
In this stillness, magic thrives,
In the ballet, winter strives.

Glimmering Silence

In the stillness, stars ignite,
Whispers glow in the velvet night.
Moonlight spills like silver streams,
Chasing shadows, weaving dreams.

Silence hums, a gentle song,
Where the echoes of life belong.
Every heartbeat, soft and clear,
In the glimmer, we draw near.

Thoughts like lanterns, glowing bright,
Guide us through the endless night.
In the calm, we find our way,
In the silence, night turns to day.

With every breath, the world holds tight,
Glimmers dance in the soft twilight.
Peace enfolds in a warm embrace,
In this silence, we find our place.

As dawn awakens, hues will blend,
All the glimmering dreams will tend.
Yet in silence, we now know,
It's in the quiet that we grow.

Melancholy in Frost

Morning's breath, a whispered chill,
Branches bare, the world stands still.
Footsteps muffled, echoes lost,
Underneath the silver frost.

Shadows stretch, the daylight fades,
A quiet touch, the heart persuades.
Leaves like whispers, crisp and hush,
Nature wears her somber blush.

Frozen lakes, reflections dim,
Haunting thoughts in dusk's soft hymn.
Echoed sighs of dreams once dear,
Drown in silence, thick with fear.

Clouds embrace the waning sun,
Daylight's warmth, a race undone.
Time meanders, bittersweet,
In this frost, a friend we meet.

Memories trace the icy night,
Fleeting shadows, ghostly light.
Melancholy's grip, it lingers,
Wrapped in frost with ghostly fingers.

Sighs of the Silent Season

Winter whispers on the breeze,
Frosted stories, hidden needs.
Trees remain in solemn grace,
Kissing earth with frozen face.

Snowflakes tumble, soft and light,
Glimmers dance through fading night.
Past the windows, shadows play,
In the quiet, thoughts decay.

Moonlight drapes a silver shroud,
Echoes form a ghostly crowd.
Hopeful hearts held tight with fear,
In the silence, secrets leer.

Stars above, like distant dreams,
Fill the dark with muted gleams.
Sighs escape the frozen lips,
As the season slowly slips.

Embers fade in waning light,
Yearning warms the coldest night.
Within stillness, life's refrain,
Sighs of longing, soft as rain.

Reverberations of the Pale Light

Pale sun rises, casting glow,
Mist unfolds, the world moves slow.
Hope emerges from shadow's bind,
In the soft light, peace we find.

Waves of silence, whispers vast,
Epochs pass, like shadows cast.
Wind sings softly through the trees,
Carrying tales upon the breeze.

Echoes of a fleeting past,
Time's embrace is ever vast.
Reverberating through the night,
Not a soul can halt its flight.

Moonlit paths, a ghostly dance,
Stars collide in a cosmic trance.
Each heartbeat echoes in the dark,
Fleeting moments leave their mark.

In the stillness, dreams take flight,
Painted softly by pale light.
Boundless realms where shadows play,
Reverberations fade away.

Shivers in Stillness

Stillness drapes the evening air,
Fingers numb from winter's care.
Shivers dance upon my skin,
A gentle touch where thoughts begin.

Candles flicker, shadows creep,
In the quiet, secrets sleep.
Whispers thread through darkened night,
Wrapped in warmth, we chase the light.

Snowflakes fall, a silent kiss,
Moments caught in endless bliss.
Underneath the night's soft wing,
Life's reflections softly sing.

Frosted windows tell a tale,
Of love and dreams that shall prevail.
In the heart, a fire glows,
Guiding through where stillness grows.

Breath held tight in frozen air,
Each heartbeat is beyond compare.
Shivers warm when spirits rise,
In stillness, endless skies.

The Lullaby of January

Winter whispers soft and low,
Blankets of white, a gentle glow.
Stars adorn the velvet night,
Dreams take wing on frosty light.

Fires crackle, warmth we share,
In this stillness, hearts lay bare.
Snowflakes dance like drifting sighs,
Each moment blessed, as time flies.

Silent shadows softly creep,
Nature sighs, it seems asleep.
Yet in the hush, the world spins on,
A lullaby till break of dawn.

Children laugh and build their dreams,
In the snow, a world redeems.
Each footstep leaves a story told,
In every flake, a wish of old.

January nights, a magic spell,
With tales of quiet weaves to tell.
So hold this moment, let it stay,
In the lullaby of yesterday.

Snowbound Reveries

The world is hushed in silvery light,
Every branch wrapped, a beautiful sight.
Footprints trace paths on blankets of white,
In this silence, all feels right.

Clouds drift softly, a soft embrace,
Time slows down in this tranquil space.
Whispers of winter, a gentle chime,
Within these moments, we pause time.

Candles flicker, shadows play,
Stories linger in warm array.
Fires glow with embers bright,
Filling the heart with pure delight.

Outside, the drifts reach high and steep,
As dreams and wishes start to leap.
In every swirl, a tale is spun,
Snowbound reveries, all in fun.

As night unfolds, the stars awake,
A frosty quilt, the earth's own make.
Lost in wonder, we find our way,
In snowbound dreams that softly sway.

Frostbitten Cantata

A symphony sung in crisp, cold air,
Each note, a flake, delicate and rare.
Wind carries melodies high and free,
Nature's chorus, a frozen decree.

Branches adorned in sparkling lace,
Every glimmer a fleeting grace.
In the hush, the world takes pause,
Listening close to winter's cause.

Voices of silence wrap around,
In the frost, a beauty profound.
Each chill breath, a story told,
In the cantata of winter's hold.

Snow falls soft, a gentle touch,
Wrapping the earth in peace, so much.
Each echo dances, a joyful play,
In nature's harmony, night or day.

So let us sing, our hearts unite,
In this season, pure and bright.
A frostbitten cantata, sweet and clear,
In every heartbeat, winter's cheer.

Crystal Chimes

Through the trees, a soft wind blows,
Bells of winter in silence propose.
They jingle softly, a gentle rhyme,
Echoing through, like childhood time.

Icicles hang like frozen tears,
Reflecting light, dispelling fears.
Each glint a memory, bright and fine,
In the dance of the crystal chime.

Outside the window, the world aglow,
Fields of white, a tranquil flow.
Hearts entwined in warmth and cheer,
Filling our souls as winter draws near.

As snowflakes settle, the world transforms,
In frosted beauty, a calm that warms.
Every chime sings a lullaby fair,
Bathing our spirits in crisp, clean air.

So let us wander in this delight,
Hand in hand, through the stars of night.
With every moment, let's take our time,
In the magic of the crystal chime.

Shadows of the Falling Snow

A whisper falls upon the ground,
As shadows dance, they swirl around.
Each flake a story, silent and bright,
In winter's hush, they claim the night.

Branches droop with heavy sighs,
Underneath the silver skies.
Footsteps muffled, soft and slow,
In the silence, dreams can grow.

The world adorned in purest white,
Transforming dark to softest light.
Echoes linger, time stands still,
In frosted air, a cherished thrill.

Moonbeams cast a gentle glow,
On every branch, on every bow.
A tapestry of winter's grace,
In the shadows, we find our place.

Underneath the stars we wait,
For beauty shared; we celebrate.
Together here, no fear to tread,
In falling snow, our hearts are led.

Serenity of a Frozen World

Amidst the pines, the quiet reigns,
A frozen spell, where stillness gains.
Each breath of air, a frosty sigh,
In winter's clutch, the moments lie.

The world transformed in silver lace,
Time slows down, a warm embrace.
Whispers of peace, the cold ignites,
As stars above illuminate nights.

Crisp and clear, the landscape glows,
In every shimmer, beauty flows.
A gentle touch, the snowflakes kiss,
In quiet realms, we find our bliss.

With every step, the crunch of sound,
Like fleeting dreams from underground.
Each heart beats slow, in rhythm found,
In this serene, enchanted ground.

Beneath the sky, a world reborn,
Wrapped in white, the day is sworn.
Here in stillness, we come alive,
In the frozen realm, we thrive.

Breaths of a Snowy Dawn

As dawn breaks soft, the world awakes,
In hues of pink where silence makes.
Snow blankets earth in gentle glow,
A quiet start where soft winds blow.

The air is crisp, a soothing balm,
In winter's breath, a perfect calm.
With golden rays, the sun ascends,
And paints the frost where magic blends.

Trees adorned with diamonds bright,
Sparkling jewels in morning light.
Each branch a canvas, nature's art,
In every flutter, warmth imparts.

Footsteps whisper on the trail,
While whispers weave a tender tale.
In this snowy realm, we pause,
And give our hearts a moment's cause.

The dawn unfolds, a canvas clear,
A masterpiece for all to cheer.
In breaths of snow, our spirits soar,
In every flake, we find much more.

Compositions of the Frostbite

In every breath, the chill persists,
A melody in winter's mist.
The air so sharp, it sings with light,
Composed in notes of frost and flight.

Each flake a note that softly lands,
On silent fields, on frozen strands.
Together forming symphonies,
In harmonies that ride the breeze.

A tapestry of white and grey,
Where beauty shines in cold array.
Nature's brush paints all around,
In every droplet, magic found.

Through crystal sights, the world reborn,
New compositions, fresh and warm.
Each frosty touch a fleeting kiss,
In winter's hold, we find our bliss.

The world around a quiet score,
As frozen time reveals much more.
In compositions, hearts ignite,
In frosty realms, we write our light.

Twilight Under a Blanket of Snow

The sun slips low, a fading glow,
Each flake descends, as soft winds blow.
Whispers of night fill the cold air,
A silver hush, a world laid bare.

Trees stand still, draped in white,
Branches flicker in fading light.
Footsteps hush on the frozen ground,
In this silence, peace is found.

Stars awaken in the deepening sky,
As shadows dance, and night draws nigh.
Underneath, the soft snow gleams,
Wrapped in dreams, we drift in dreams.

The world transforms at nature's hand,
In twilight's grip, we understand.
Moments cherished, lost in time,
Bathed in beauty, pure and sublime.

As I gaze, my heart takes flight,
In a world of wonder, pure delight.
Twilight whispers, peaceful and slow,
Beneath the stars, we linger low.

The Breath of December

December breathes, a frosty sigh,
Leaves lie down as they crumple dry.
Winter's chill wraps the barren trees,
A shift in time, a gentle freeze.

Candles flicker, warm embers glow,
While outside, the cold winds blow.
Hot cocoa warms each eager hand,
Hushed giggles echo through the land.

The nights grow long, the days are brief,
In its grasp, we find some relief.
Cozy blankets, firelight's dance,
In December's arms, we find our chance.

Silent evenings, moonlight's gleam,
Woven dreams like a soft, warm seam.
With every breath, we hold the cold,
As stories of winter gently unfold.

As the month wanes and transitions near,
Memories linger, precious and dear.
Wrapped in warmth, we'll cherish the breath,
Of December's beauty, life in depth.

A Wintry Composition

Snowflakes twirl like notes in flight,
A symphony born of winter's night.
Whirling softly, they dance around,
Composing magic without a sound.

Every drift tells a tale of old,
Of laughter and warmth, of hearts so bold.
As children play, they sculpt their dreams,
In nature's canvas, life redeems.

Branches wear their frosty lace,
Each moment etched in time and space.
The world adorned in white and blue,
A masterpiece of fiery hue.

Chilling winds breathe life anew,
In each flake, a hope breaks through.
Frozen pools reflect the sky,
As winter's song flows gently by.

As dusk descends, the skies ignite,
A wintry verse in the fading light.
So let us linger, hand in hand,
A composition we can understand.

Serenading the Chill

In the hushed glow, the cold invades,
The world alights in winter shades.
Where once was warmth, now silence stands,
Serenading chill across the lands.

Frosty breaths mingle with the air,
A whispered sigh, a moment rare.
Shadows stretch on the silver ground,
As twilight's dusk softly surrounds.

Each step crunches on the frozen earth,
Echoes of laughter, warmth, and mirth.
The chill wraps tight like a soft embrace,
In this serene and sacred place.

As stars appear, they sing their tune,
A ballad bright beneath the moon.
Nature's whispers fill the night,
Guiding hearts with gentle light.

So let us breathe in the frosty air,
In winter's chill, we find our prayer.
As music swells from the mountain's height,
We dance with shadows, lost in the night.

Frosty Tides

The ocean breathes in icy sighs,
Where frosty waves meet winter skies.
The moonlight dances on the shore,
Whispers of tales from days of yore.

Seagulls call in the crisp, cold air,
Fleeting shadows of dreams laid bare.
The horizon glows with twilight's charm,
Nature's beauty, a serene calm.

Waves crash gently, a lullaby,
Beneath the vast and starry sky.
Footprints fade in the powdery snow,
As the tide recedes, the winds do blow.

Frosty trails where the seabirds roam,
Carved by ages, they call it home.
Each ripple tells a story untold,
Of secrets hidden, both new and old.

In the silence, magic unfolds,
As the sea embraces the cold.
Time stands still, a fleeting bliss,
In the frosty tide's gentle kiss.

Lullabies of the Northern Wind

Softly whispers the northern breeze,
Carrying dreams through ancient trees.
Stars above like gems in a thread,
Guiding our hearts where spirits tread.

Veils of snow cover the hill,
With a quiet peace, the world is still.
Crickets sing their nightly tune,
As shadows dance 'neath the watchful moon.

Lullabies drift on frigid air,
Murmurs of love in a world so rare.
The silence sings beneath the night,
As nature weaves her soft, soft light.

Frosty breath in the crystal skies,
Where a million wishes softly rise.
The echoes of history gently sway,
In the arms of night, we lose our way.

Dreamers gather beneath the stars,
With hopes and wishes, it heals our scars.
In the stillness, hearts intertwine,
With lullabies of the northern pine.

Icy Visions

Reflections shimmer on the frozen lake,
Where whispering winds, still silence break.
The world transforms in pearly white,
As icy visions fill the night.

A moonlit path on gleaming snow,
Leads hidden spirits, both high and low.
In that glow, all secrets hide,
Beneath the frost, hearts confide.

Glistening stars on blankets of blue,
Carry the hopes of the brave and true.
In this wonderland, dreams ignite,
With icy visions, we take flight.

The trees stand guard, their branches bare,
Nature's breath hangs in the cold air.
Each crystal shard, a wish reborn,
In the still night, where dreams are worn.

Awake, we breathe this tranquil scene,
Lost in the magic, soft and serene.
With icy visions, the world seems bright,
In the heart of winter's endless night.

Threads of Silver in the Twilight

In twilight's glow, threads of silver spin,
Weaving tales as the stars begin.
With every twinkle, a story unfolds,
Of love and dreams, both brave and bold.

Whispers of dusk brush the silent trees,
Carrying secrets on the evening breeze.
Soft shadows dance like fleeting time,
In the quiet night, a gentle rhyme.

A silver moon in a velvet sky,
Calls on hearts that wander by.
Each star a beacon, guiding dreams,
In the twilight's hold, nothing is as it seems.

Threads of silver wrap the night,
Cradling hopes in their tender light.
With every heartbeat, they softly guide,
The wandering souls that seek to confide.

As the darkness deepens and night takes flight,
We find our peace in the soft twilight.
The world transformed in a soothing glow,
With threads of silver, our spirits flow.

Shadows in the Glimmer

Whispers dance in the twilight,
Flickering stars in the night,
Shadows sway with a shimmer,
Guided by the moon's light.

Echoes of dreams softly fade,
Carried on winds of delight,
In the depths, secrets are laid,
Enigmas found in the night.

Glimmers paint the dark skies,
With silver threads of the stars,
Illuminating our sighs,
In the realm of dreams and scars.

Silent visions begin to unfold,
Murmurs of tales long forgot,
Each story, a treasure to hold,
In the glimmer of what we sought.

As dawn's light begins to creep,
Shadows melt with the sun,
Awakening from the deep,
The night's magic is done.

The Lull of the Long Nights

Stars twinkle in the velvet dome,
Cocooned in the softest night,
Every shadow feels like home,
Whispers woven with moonlight.

Crickets serenade the dark,
Lullabies in the still air,
Their echoes ignite a spark,
Cradling dreams to softly share.

Gentle breezes caress the skin,
While fireflies dance in delight,
The calmness beckons us in,
Sheltered by the cloak of night.

Moments linger, time stands still,
In the hush of the night's embrace,
Hearts align with a gentle thrill,
Lost in the silence, we trace.

As dawn slowly peeks its head,
Replacing stars with glowing hues,
We rise from the dreams we've fed,
Carrying the night's warm muse.

Tranquil Trills

In the morning's tender light,
Birds begin their soft refrain,
Trills weave through the air so bright,
Nature's music, pure and plain.

Leaves rustle in gentle sighs,
Carried by the wakeful breeze,
Every sound, a sweet surprise,
Whispers shared among the trees.

The brook sings a soothing beat,
Flowing with a rhythmic grace,
Droplets dance to nature's heat,
Every ripple leaves a trace.

Mountains echo with their might,
Resonating deep within,
A symphony of pure delight,
Where silence meets the din.

As twilight casts its golden hue,
The world hushes, comes alive,
Tranquil trills create anew,
In harmony, we all thrive.

Chilling Harmonies

Frosty winds whisper secrets,
Sculpting breath in crystal air,
Nature's pulse, a sharp duet,
Echoes shiver everywhere.

Moonlight bathes the fields in white,
Casting shadows, deep and long,
Each step feels crisp and light,
As the night hums its chill song.

Harmonies of the quiet night,
Ribbons of cold seep through trees,
They carry both fear and delight,
Unknown paths in swirling breeze.

With every note, the heart races,
In the dark, a thrill ignites,
Wandering through enchanted places,
Trapped in chilling, dreamy sights.

As daylight cracks the icy shell,
And warmth blankets the frozen ground,
We ride the waves of the spell,
From harmony, new hope is found.

Muffled Footsteps on Ice

A whisper of snow beneath my feet,
Shadows dance where silence meets.
The world holds its breath in the chill,
Only the heart's pulse, loud and still.

Frosted branches lean with grace,
Nature dons a crystal lace.
Every step a gentle sigh,
As winter wanes, the echoes lie.

Footprints trace a fleeting line,
Memory wrapped in icy twine.
Each echo carries a tale untold,
In the frozen air, warmth unfolds.

The stillness sings a solemn song,
Where the night whispers, we belong.
With every breath, the chill ignites,
Muffled footsteps on starry nights.

Crystalline Verses

In twilight's grasp, a shimmer bright,
Words like snowflakes dance in flight.
Each verse a gem, pure and rare,
Crafted in the winter air.

Ink flows cold on parchment white,
Beneath the stars, in soft moonlight.
Thoughts crystallize in gentle flows,
A tapestry of timeless prose.

Whispers echo, soft and clear,
Frozen thoughts, held so dear.
In every line, a world contained,
In icy beauty, love unchained.

Each stanza shimmers, glitters bright,
A symphony of pure delight.
Crafted with care, like snow on eaves,
Crystalline verses that no one leaves.

Embracing quiet, calm, and peace,
In the winter's grasp, thoughts release.
As pages turn, the feelings bloom,
In crystalline verses, the heart finds room.

Resounding Quietude

In the stillness, shadows play,
Echoes linger, drift away.
The soft hum of nature's pause,
Moments held without a cause.

Silent whispers, gentle breeze,
Rustling leaves in peaceful trees.
Time stands still in twilight's glow,
Where the world moves soft and slow.

Each heartbeat resonates with song,
In quietude, we all belong.
A symphony of muted sounds,
In serene calm, the soul surrounds.

The absence of noise speaks so loud,
In tranquil spaces, we are proud.
Lost in thought, finding our way,
In resounding quietude, we stay.

Moments linger, soft and sweet,
In stillness found, our hearts repeat.
With every breath, peace we seed,
In the quiet, we are freed.

The Beauty of Brisk Air

Crisp and clear, the morning calls,
A whispering breath as daylight falls.
Each gust a kiss on rosy cheeks,
Nature speaks in chilling peaks.

Eager spirits bound to roam,
Finding warmth in fields we know.
Breath visible in frosty air,
Moments linger, light as prayer.

Chasing shadows, leaping high,
Where frostbitten dreams dare to fly.
The beauty of now, in every breath,
Alive with the thrill of fleeting sets.

Joy abounds in the cold embrace,
In brisk air's hold, we find our place.
Each step a dance, each laugh a song,
In the beauty of brisk air, we belong.

Underneath a pale blue sky,
With every exhale, spirits fly.
Together we weave, hearts aglow,
In the brisk air, forever flow.

A Palette of Frost

Winter's breath paints the trees,
Colors drawn from dreams with ease.
A canvas white, a world anew,
A palette rich in frozen hue.

Glittering crystals catch the light,
Sparkling jewels, a dazzling sight.
Nature's brush strokes bold and fine,
In every flake, a love divine.

Soft whispers float on chilly air,
Each breath leaves behind a fleeting glare.
A world wrapped tight in frosty lace,
Every corner, a cold embrace.

In silence, beauty slowly grows,
A quiet peace, the stillness shows.
Each moment held, a fleeting glance,
Life's icy breath in a quiet dance.

Underneath the starry skies,
The moonlight casts its silver sighs.
Frosty nights hold secrets deep,
In nature's arms, we softly sleep.

The Silence Between the Flakes

Falling softly, the snow descends,
Wrapping the world like timeless friends.
In the hush, a gentle grace,
The silence holds a warm embrace.

Each flake whispers a secret tale,
In the still, where echoes pale.
A quiet calm, the heartbeats sync,
In this moment, we stop to think.

Shadows dance on the blanket white,
Lost in thoughts that take their flight.
Breath of winter, crisp and clear,
The silence hums, drawing near.

Frosted branches sway and bend,
Nature breathes, a timeless friend.
Wrapped in comfort, we draw close,
Finding warmth in frost's soft prose.

With every flake, a wish we send,
In the quiet, our hearts mend.
The silence sings a soothing song,
In winter's arms, where we belong.

Syllables in the Chill

A shivering night, the stars ignite,
Whispers of snow take gentle flight.
Syllables soft in frigid air,
Every breath a frosty prayer.

Words unspoken find their way,
In winter's grasp, they gently sway.
Each heartbeat echoes, calm and slow,
In this stillness, memories flow.

The world transformed, a quiet scene,
Where shadows linger, almost serene.
In icy verses, stories freeze,
Captured moments, hearts at ease.

Tender flakes weave tales so bright,
Dancing softly in the night.
A symphony of chill and grace,
Every syllable finds its place.

Underneath the frozen glow,
We gather warmth, let our love show.
This wintry tapestry we find,
In syllables, our souls aligned.

Twilight's Icy Kiss

When twilight drapes the world in grey,
Frosted edges softly play.
An icy kiss upon the skin,
Whispers of night, the day grows thin.

Shadows stretch with a graceful sigh,
As sunlight bids the day goodbye.
Each moment crisp, a fleeting bliss,
Caught in time's most gentle kiss.

Silver skies hold a quiet tune,
In the hush beneath the moon.
Every flake joins in the dance,
Embracing winter's soft romance.

Beneath the chill, the hearts ignite,
With dreams awakened in the night.
In twilight's arms, we find our place,
Lost in love's embrace, a warm space.

As stars emerge, the world holds still,
In icy whispers, we feel the thrill.
Twilight's kiss, a promise made,
In winter's heart, we softly wade.

Symphony of Solitude

In shadows deep, I find my peace,
The world unheard, a sweet release.
Each echo sings a tender tone,
In silence, I am not alone.

With whispered thoughts that softly flow,
I dance with dreams, the night aglow.
The moonlit path, a guiding light,
In solitude, I take my flight.

The stars entwined, a cosmic thread,
In stillness, countless tales are spread.
A symphony of heart and mind,
In every note, my soul aligned.

Each heartbeat syncs with every breath,
In quietude, I find no death.
For in this space, I learn to grow,
A garden where my spirit flows.

Embracing shadows, I feel whole,
In solitude, I find my soul.
A symphony that plays for me,
In every chord, I feel so free.

Whispers in White

The snowflakes fall, a soft embrace,
They cloak the world in quiet grace.
Each flake a story, light and bright,
Whispers in white, a pure delight.

The trees stand tall with branches bare,
In frosty air, they greet the glare.
A tranquil hush blankets the night,
A silent dance, a dream in sight.

The moon peeks through, a silver gleam,
Beside the frost, it casts a dream.
With every drift, new tales in thrall,
Each whisper beckons, hear their call.

In winter's hold, the heart feels warm,
Through icy winds, we feel the charm.
Each step leaves prints, an artist's mark,
A fleeting trace in twilight's dark.

The world transforms, a canvas bright,
In gentle strokes of purest white.
Through whispers soft, I find my song,
In snowy realms, we all belong.

Glistening Verses

Upon the page, the words do dance,
In glistening hues, they weave a trance.
Each line a path, a journey spun,
In written light, our tales are done.

The ink flows bright, a river's might,
With every turn, there's pure delight.
Like morning dew on blades of grass,
In verses glinting, moments pass.

The rhythm beats, a heart in song,
In glistening words, we all belong.
Each stanza shines, a radiant kiss,
In poetry, we find our bliss.

The pages turn, a lover's sigh,
In whispered dreams, our spirits fly.
Each verse a spark, a fluttered heart,
In glistening verses, we play our part.

Embrace the light, the words ignite,
In every rhyme, make darkness bright.
With glistening ink, our worlds unite,
In poetry's arms, we feel the light.

A Blanket of Stillness

In twilight's arms, the day does rest,
A blanket soft, the night is best.
With stars like gems in velvet skies,
A stillness wraps where silence lies.

The wind whispers secrets, low and sweet,
In shadows long, the echoes meet.
The world slows down, a gentle sigh,
As nighttime paints the land awry.

Each moment pauses, time stands still,
In tranquil thoughts, we find the thrill.
A blanket woven, dreams take flight,
In stillness deep, we greet the night.

The moonlight drapes a silver sheet,
Upon the earth, a calm retreat.
In quiet hours, our hearts explore,
A blanket of peace forevermore.

With every breath, the night unfolds,
In whispered dreams, our stories told.
A blanket of stillness, warm embrace,
In nighttime's glow, we find our place.

Frosted Whispers

In the hush of winter's breath,
Soft whispers weave through the trees.
Each flake a tale of gentle death,
Kissing the ground with quiet ease.

Moonlight dances on icy streams,
Stars twinkle like forgotten dreams.
The world in stillness, wrapped in white,
Glows softly under the silver light.

Branches bow with a crystal weight,
Nature's beauty, swift and great.
Frozen echoes fill the air,
A tranquil moment, pure and rare.

Footprints lead to hidden paths,
Where secrets lie beneath the snow.
Every step, a whispered laugh,
As winter nights begin to glow.

Beneath the veil, life waits and sighs,
For warmer days to come anew.
Yet in this frost, a fleeting prize,
With every breath, the world feels true.

Melodies of Snowflakes

Softly falling, flakes of white,
Singing songs of winter's grace.
Each one unique, a pure delight,
In the silence, they embrace.

Harmonies swirl in cool night air,
Nature's choir, a gentle sound.
Lifting spirits, without a care,
As snowflakes drift upon the ground.

Underfoot, they whisper low,
Stories of where they long have been.
A melody produced by snow,
Echoes of winter, soft and clean.

Stars above twinkle in delight,
Joining in this peaceful song.
The world is wrapped in cozy light,
As winter nights sweep all along.

Joy flows freely in this cold,
Each note a pause, a fleeting cheer.
In the air, the warmth unfolds,
Melodies to hold forever near.

Echoes in the Chill

In the chill of midnight air,
Echoes dance on frosty ground.
Whispers weave through silence there,
Softly murmurs all around.

Frozen branches creak and sigh,
As shadows play on moonlit snow.
A frosty breeze begins to fly,
Carrying tales from long ago.

Footfalls silent, hearts at peace,
Nature's lullaby, soft and slow.
In the night, worries cease,
As stars above begin to glow.

Echoes linger, faint and clear,
A reminder of winter's hold.
In the crispness, there's no fear,
Only stories waiting to be told.

Underneath the silver sky,
The chill wraps around like a shawl.
In the stillness, spirits fly,
Embracing winter's loving call.

Harmonics of the Frozen Night

The frozen night sings low and sweet,
With harmonics softly spread.
Every shadow, winter's feat,
A world of white, a dreamlike bed.

Stars align in cosmic dance,
Beneath the chill, hearts intertwine.
Each breath, a whispered chance,
To find solace in the divine.

Winds carry notes from faraway,
Melodies wrapped in snowflakes' grace.
A nightingale, its song at play,
Hiding 'neath the winter's face.

Gentle rhythms softly creep,
Through the quiet, peaceful night.
Nature's chorus, secrets keep,
As fading echoes take their flight.

In this moment, time stands still,
Wrapped in clouds of frosty breath.
The harmony, a soothing thrill,
Awakens dreams of warmth from death.

A Canvas of Ice

The world is draped in silver light,
Each crystal whispers, pure and bright.
Trees wear coats of frosted lace,
In winter's grip, we find our place.

Footprints mark the snowy ground,
Every step a gentle sound.
A canvas stretches, white and wide,
Nature's art, we cannot hide.

Icicles dangle, sharp and clear,
Nature's daggers, cold and near.
Each breath a cloud that drifts away,
In this realm, we long to stay.

The frozen lake reflects the sky,
A mirror where our dreams can fly.
Children laugh, their joy so keen,
In this landscape, pure and serene.

As twilight falls, the stars ignite,
Guiding us through the endless night.
In a cold embrace, we find our warmth,
In this canvas, we shall transform.

Sonnet of the Subzero

In winter's breath, a frosty chill,
The air is sharp, the world stands still.
Each flake that falls, a gentle sigh,
Subzero dreams beneath the sky.

The night is deep, the stars alight,
A tapestry of pure delight.
Underneath this frozen dome,
We find in coldness, our true home.

The silence speaks, a haunting song,
In these still moments, we belong.
With every breath, a tale we weave,
In nature's hold, we choose to believe.

So let the winds of winter blow,
Through icy paths, let our hearts grow.
For in the subzero's sweet embrace,
We find our strength, our truest grace.

Rhythms of Restful Slumber

As dusk descends, the world slows down,
Whispers linger, without a sound.
Beneath the quilt of starry skies,
Nature sighs, and silence lies.

The moonlight dances on the lake,
Every wave, a soft-heartbreak.
In shadows deep, our dreams take flight,
Restful slumber, through the night.

Crickets sing their lullabies,
Gentle breezes, a soft reprise.
In the dark, the world enchants,
As sleep invites our weary chants.

The night unfolds its calming grace,
In its embrace, we find our space.
With every heartbeat, rhythms blend,
A timeless melody, never ends.

Awake to dawn's light-breaking beams,
In this calm, we weave our dreams.
Restful slumber leads the way,
To greet the warmth of a new day.

Whirlwind of Chill

A storm descends, the winds arise,
Whirling clouds obscure the skies.
Nature spins, a dance of frost,
In this chill, we count the cost.

Branches sway, the trees will bend,
In this whirlwind, we must transcend.
Snowflakes swirl like dreams untold,
Wrapped in warmth, we brave the cold.

Each gust a song of winter's might,
A chilling breath that sparks the night.
Through swirling drifts, we find our way,
In nature's game, we choose to play.

The tempest rages, fierce and bold,
Yet in our hearts, we find a gold.
For in the storm, a magic lies,
A whirlwind where our spirit flies.

When calm returns, the world is still,
We've danced with frost, we've felt the thrill.
In the aftermath, the quiet speaks,
Of winter's grace and spring's warm peaks.

Echoes of the Iced Earth

Whispers beneath the frozen ground,
Silent tales that time has crowned.
Shadows dance on crystal spires,
A world consumed by winter's fires.

Frosty breath on ancient stone,
Echoes of life, now overthrown.
Nature's pulse a distant dream,
In the ice, a haunting gleam.

Birches wrapped in delicate white,
Stand like sentinels in the night.
Footfalls muffled, they drift away,
In the stillness, lost to the day.

Glaciers hum soft lullabies,
Beneath the vast and starry skies.
A tapestry of silence gleams,
As daylight fades, night softly dreams.

Beneath the frost, the past survives,
In each crack, the heartbeat thrives.
Echoes linger, soft and near,
In the ice, memories appear.

Muffled Songs of the Sky

Clouds drifting in a hazy blue,
Muffled songs, both old and new.
Wind carries whispers on its wings,
As day breaks, the silence sings.

Frost forms patterns on the glass,
Time weaves through moments that pass.
Songs of twilight, soft and light,
Fade into the arms of night.

Stars shimmer in the vast expanse,
Nighttime offers a hushed dance.
Underneath the moon's soft glow,
Muffled dreams begin to flow.

The sky holds stories, still untold,
In every hue, in every fold.
A symphony of silence reigns,
In the calm before the rains.

Muffled songs like gentle sighs,
Float through dark, embracing skies.
Each note a promise, soft and clear,
In the stillness, echoes near.

Brushstrokes of Cold

Winter paints with icy breath,
A canvas kissed by quiet death.
Each stroke a chill, each hue a sigh,
In the stillness, dreams pass by.

Pine trees wrapped in layers white,
Stand like ghosts in fading light.
A world transformed, both stark and bright,
Where shadows linger, out of sight.

Snowflakes twirl, a dance divine,
Each one unique, a fleeting sign.
Whispers carried on the breeze,
Nature's brush on frozen leaves.

Brushstrokes merge in twilight's hue,
A monochrome, yet vivid view.
The earth wears frost as a crown,
In quietude, it settles down.

The palette speaks in hush and glow,
Of stories told in winter's flow.
Through every line, through every fold,
Life persists in brushstrokes cold.

Rhapsody of the Frozen Landscape

In a rhapsody of ice and snow,
Nature's symphony begins to flow.
Harmony sings in each crisp note,
As winter's rhythm bids us float.

Mountains echo with frozen grace,
Time suspends in this quiet place.
Every flake a part of the song,
In the silence, we belong.

Rivers wrapped in a frosty embrace,
Reflect the heavens, a timeless space.
Each glimmer speaks of stories lost,
In the chill, we count the cost.

Footsteps trace where fear once lay,
In the shadows, we find our way.
The landscape whispers tales untold,
In the rhapsody, our hearts unfold.

With each exhale, the beauty grows,
In the stillness, the magic flows.
This frozen dream forever stays,
In whispers soft, in winter's gaze.

Lullabies Under the Moonlight

Soft whispers in the night,
Stars twinkle with delight.
Crickets sing a gentle tune,
Dreams are woven by the moon.

In the hush, the shadows creep,
Cradling all those fast asleep.
A lullaby of silver beams,
Guiding us through tender dreams.

Moonlight spills on silent streams,
Stirring thoughts of peaceful themes.
Every breath, a soft embrace,
Wrapped in night's enchanting grace.

With each sigh, the world grows still,
The heart finds solace in goodwill.
Nature whispers secrets low,
In the glow, sweet calm will grow.

As night fades, dawn will break,
But these lullabies will wake.
Memories of moonlit skies,
Forever held where starlight lies.

Dance of the Winter Winds

Whispers dart through icy trees,
Carrying a chill with ease.
Snowflakes swirl in graceful flight,
Dancing softly in the night.

Branches sway, a gentle sway,
Winter winds come out to play.
A frosty breath upon my skin,
The season's song begins to spin.

Footsteps crunch on frozen ground,
Magic lingers all around.
Echoes of a world so bright,
In the dance of winter's light.

Through the pines, the breezes glide,
Nature's rhythm, wild and wide.
A symphony of cold and grace,
In this winter's warm embrace.

Stars peek out from skies of grey,
Guiding us through night and day.
With every gust that softly calls,
The winter's dance, it never stalls.

Notes from the Icy Abyss

Deep beneath the frozen sea,
Whispers echo, wild and free.
Shadows dance in watery halls,
Nature's symphony enthralls.

Glacial cracks create a song,
Resonating deep and strong.
Creatures drift in silent flows,
In the depths where no light glows.

Bubbles rise like dreams set free,
Carried forth by currents' plea.
An underwater ballet blooms,
In the midst of icy tombs.

Notes of solitude and grace,
Paint the dark with a soft trace.
Time stands still in liquid blue,
Where the past and present strew.

Hear the secrets of the deep,
In the abyss, the ancients sleep.
Every wave a story told,
In whispers of the deep and cold.

Twilight's Gentle Embrace

The sun dips low, a golden hue,
Painting skies in shades so true.
Nighttime dances on the edge,
A whisper soft, a fleeting pledge.

Shadows stretch and colors fade,
In twilight's warm and tender shade.
Fireflies flicker, stars ignite,
As day surrenders to the night.

The world is wrapped in softest light,
A moment's peace, a sweet delight.
Dreams awaken, softly trace,
In twilight's gentle, sweet embrace.

Crickets chirp a lullaby,
While the moon begins to rise.
Nature sighs in calm repose,
As twilight's beauty softly glows.

Each heartbeat syncs with passing time,
In this soft, enchanting rhyme.
Embraced by night, we find our place,
Lost forever in twilight's grace.

Icicles in Harmony

Icicles dangled from the roof,
A silent symphony of chill.
Sunlight sparkling in their tips,
Nature's beauty, calm and still.

Whispers ride the winter breeze,
Where snowflakes dance on frozen ground.
Each one tells a tale, a tease,
Of memories lost, yet so profound.

Branches bare, yet strong they stand,
Cradling crystals, pure and bright.
In the quiet of the land,
Harmony thrives in the night.

Footsteps crunch on white terrain,
Echoes of laughter fill the air.
Every breath, a fleeting pain,
A moment cherished, beyond compare.

As daylight fades, the stars appear,
A canvas painted with pure light.
Icicles shimmer, crystal clear,
In the frosty embrace of night.

Solstice Serenade

In the heart of longest night,
The world wraps in twilight's glow.
Whispers of the stars take flight,
A serenade in silent snow.

Frozen rivers gently flow,
Carving tales through ancient stone.
Nature's breath, soft and low,
In the stillness, not alone.

Crickets hush, the owls call,
Echoes dance in icy air.
Underneath the wintry thrall,
Tranquility beyond compare.

As shadows stretch and deepen wide,
The moon awakes, a silver queen.
Guiding dreams, a gentle tide,
In the stillness, pure and serene.

At dawn, the light will break anew,
Illuminating all that's here.
And in that warmth, the world will brew,
A cycle of life, year after year.

A Cold Embrace

Winter wraps the earth so tight,
A cold embrace of frozen time.
Every breath, a crystal sight,
Nature's pulse in frozen rhyme.

Trees stand proud against the sky,
Draped in white, serene and bold.
Frozen whispers softly sigh,
In the night, their stories told.

Stars flicker in the velvet dark,
Guiding spirits through the chill.
Each one leaves a tiny mark,
In the silence, hearts can fill.

Children laugh, their cheeks aglow,
Crafting dreams of snow and play.
In the cold, their spirits flow,
Igniting warmth in winter's sway.

As day breaks, soft hues ignite,
Glowing softly on the frost.
In this dance of day and night,
We find warmth in all we've lost.

Echoes of the Frost

Underneath the weeping trees,
Echoes linger, faint yet clear.
Whispers ride the winter breeze,
Every sound, a voice from here.

Footfalls crunch on icy trails,
Stories written in the snow.
Each memory gently prevails,
In the heart where dreams still grow.

A stark landscape, quiet grace,
Frosted branches stretch and bend.
In their stillness, we find space,
For the echoes that ascend.

Slumbering fields await the sun,
Resting softly, under white.
Winter's reign is far from done,
Yet beneath, the seeds of light.

With each dawn, a promise made,
As warmth seeps through the cold ground.
In time, the frost will gently fade,
And life will dance, forever bound.

Frosted Whispers

Whispers low beneath the trees,
Frosted breath in winter's freeze.
Moonlight glints on silent ground,
Nature's hush, a soothing sound.

Branches draped in icy lace,
Softly, they embrace their grace.
Dreams are woven in the air,
In the night, without a care.

Footprints marked on sparkling white,
Guiding souls through starry night.
Every step a tale to tell,
In the stillness, all is well.

Frost upon the window panes,
Sings a song of winter's reigns.
Flakes descend like feathered light,
In the quiet, hearts take flight.

As dawn breaks with golden hue,
Frosted whispers bid adieu.
Yet in dreams, they softly stay,
Winter's magic, come what may.

Chilling Melodies

Beneath the sky, the echoes play,
Chilling winds that sway and sway.
Notes of frost in twilight's glow,
Songs of winter, soft and slow.

Whirling breezes, tales they share,
Carried lightly through the air.
Nature hums a gentle tune,
Underneath the watchful moon.

Each flake falls with perfect grace,
As melodies do interlace.
Harmonies of night unfold,
Whispering secrets, brave and bold.

In the silence, hear the chime,
A lullaby transcending time.
Chilling rhythms weave the night,
In their arms, we find delight.

Every sound a story spun,
Moments fleeting, lost to none.
Chilling melodies remain,
In our hearts, they leave their stain.

Silent Nights Unfold

In the still of night, we find,
Silent thoughts that dance, unlined.
Stars above like diamonds gleam,
Whispers float on midnight's dream.

Snowflakes swirl in cosmic flight,
Blanketing the world so light.
Each branch bows, a gentle bow,
Time stands still, and here, we vow.

Serenity, the air we breathe,
In the quiet, hearts believe.
Wrapped in warmth of love's embrace,
Silent nights, our sacred space.

Laughter echoes, soft and clear,
Memories linger, drawing near.
As stars align, a promise made,
In the silence, dreams cascade.

Unfolding stories, every breath,
In this night, we conquer death.
Silent moments shine like gold,
In our souls, their warmth we hold.

The Dance of Snowflakes

In the air, a twirl and twist,
Snowflakes swirl, a fleeting mist.
Falling gently, pure and bright,
The dance of winter's pure delight.

Round and round, they spin and glide,
Nature's ballet, a wondrous ride.
Each a story, unique and small,
In their descent, they cradle all.

Silvery whispers brush the night,
Holding dreams in frosted light.
A carpet woven, soft and sweet,
Underfoot, a symphony's beat.

The world transforms with every flake,
A masterpiece that dreams would make.
Catch a glimpse of winter's grace,
In this dance, find your place.

As the moonlight softly glows,
The dance continues, ever flows.
In the quiet, hearts awake,
To the beauty that snowflakes make.

Celestial Reflections in Snow

In the quiet glow of night,
Stars gaze down from heights,
Blanketing earth in white,
Whispers of winter's delights.

Footprints dance in moonlight,
Soft echoes of laughter,
Each step a fleeting flight,
Chasing dreams ever after.

Trees wear crowns of frost,
Glittering like fine lace,
Nature's beauty embossed,
In this serene embrace.

The world holds its breath tight,
Wrapped in a crystal quilt,
A realm of purest light,
Where time stands still, built.

The night hums a soft tune,
Winds weave through the pines,
A symphony of the moon,
In these celestial designs.

The Poetry of Shivering Trees

Boughs sway with a gentle grace,
Underneath the silver sky,
They whisper secrets in their space,
To the winds that flutter by.

Leaves tremble, kissed by cold,
In an art of nature's pen,
Stories of the brave and bold,
Written in a dance again.

Branches reach for warmth's embrace,
Seeking comfort from the chill,
In the solitude, they trace,
Life's rhythms, still and still.

Frost adorns their weary form,
A cloak of crystal delight,
Swinging softly, weathered, warm,
In the echo of the night.

Each rustle is a fleeting rhyme,
Nature's verses softly spoken,
In the canvas of our time,
The trees reveal love unbroken.

Lament of the Long Nights

Whispers of shadows creep low,
As daylight fades away,
A blanket of silence does grow,
In the linger of the day.

Chill settles on weary bones,
As stars blink in soft sorrow,
Time ebbs like ancient stones,
Each moment steals tomorrow.

Windows glow with warm embrace,
But outside, the cold bites deep,
The world shrouded in dark grace,
Where even shadows seem to weep.

Voices fade like distant chimes,
Melodies lost to the void,
In this tapestry of crimes,
Where hope feels almost destroyed.

Yet in the night's embrace,
There's a promise yet to keep,
For with each darkened space,
Awakens a light to leap.

Starlit Frost

Glistening jewels on the ground,
Under the vast cosmic sweep,
Nature's wonders abound,
In silence, they quietly creep.

The air is sharp, crisp and clear,
Each breath, a cloud blown away,
In the stillness, we draw near,
To witness the dawn of day.

Frozen whispers catch the light,
As dawn breaks the icy seal,
Soft hues turn from night to bright,
A canvas of dreams surreal.

Time dances on frosted leaves,
Echoes of the starlit past,
In this magic, our heart believes,
A beauty made to last.

We walk in the morning's glow,
Chasing shadows of the night,
In the starlit frost, we know,
Life's brilliance shines so bright.

Dreamscape Beneath the Snow

In silence deep, the whispers flow,
Beneath the hush of falling snow.
Stars twinkle soft in the velvet night,
As dreams take flight in gentle white.

A canvas blank, the world renews,
With every flake, a tale ensues.
A dance of shadows, a world so bright,
Awakens hearts with pure delight.

The frozen streams, they softly sigh,
Where hopes entwine with the winter sky.
Each breath a cloud, a fleeting trace,
Of warmth and love in this cold embrace.

Moonlight glimmers on icy sheets,
As nature hums her quiet beats.
In this stillness, we find our way,
Embraced by night, we long to stay.

A symphony in the chilled air,
Music of magic, beyond compare.
The dreamscape calls, with gentle tone,
In this serene, we are not alone.

Enchanted by the Flurry

Whispers of winter, soft and light,
The flurry dances, a wondrous sight.
With every gust, the laughter swells,
As dreams unfold like delicate bells.

A child's delight in a world so bright,
The frosty air lifts spirits high.
With snowflakes swirling in joyous play,
Our hearts awaken to the day.

Branches adorned in shimmering white,
Nature's jewels, a true delight.
With every turn, the enchantment grows,
In a ballet where stillness flows.

Hot cocoa warming in weary hands,
As we wander through these frozen lands.
With laughter echoing, we find our place,
In the flurry's embrace, we find our grace.

The evening falls, a hush descends,
Under the blanket, our hearts will mend.
In moonlight's glow, we dream and sigh,
Enchanted beings, through night we fly.

Echoes of the Longest Night

The longest night, with secrets deep,
Where shadows linger, and silence weeps.
Stars like lanterns, flickering bright,
Guide lost souls through the velvet night.

Mysteries whispered on the chill,
In the quiet, we find our will.
Each breath a promise, each sigh a song,
In echoes of night, where we belong.

The world at rest, a timeless dream,
Darkness softens with silver gleam.
Memories linger, swirling around,
In the heart's chamber, wisdom is found.

As dawn approaches with tender grace,
We welcome light in this sacred space.
The longest night now fades away,
Revealing hopes of a brighter day.

With every star that dims its light,
Comes the birth of a brand new sight.
In the echoes, a gentle tease,
Of warmth and promise in winter's freeze.

Frost-kissed Melodies

In winter's hush, the world holds sway,
Frost-kissed whispers, come out to play.
The trees adorned in crystalline cheer,
Sing melodies only we can hear.

Each flake a note, a soft refrain,
As they settle down on the frozen plain.
The air is crisp, the atmosphere glows,
With songs of winter, a harmony flows.

In twilight's embrace, when shadows blend,
Nature's chorus sings without end.
The quiet magic of winter's night,
Wraps around us, holding us tight.

A symphony sung by the rustling leaves,
Intertwined tales that the heart believes.
With every breath, we join the tune,
In frosty nights beneath the moon.

So let us dance through the shimmering frost,
In every note, we find what's lost.
Frost-kissed melodies guide our way,
Through winter's song, we'll always stay.

A Tapestry of Frost

A silver veil lays quiet on the ground,
Whispers of winter in the air abound.
Each flake is woven with the night's embrace,
Nature's art, a frozen, delicate grace.

Branches wear crystals, sparkling bright,
Like stars adorning the cloak of night.
Stillness reigns, in a world so vast,
Time pauses gently, forgetting the past.

Footsteps crunch on this icy stage,
A dance of shadows on a frosty page.
Breath rises softly in the chilled air,
An echo of warmth that lingers there.

Nature's breath slows, a heartbeat so fast,
In the tapestry of frost, moments are cast.
The world is hushed, secrets held tight,
In the embrace of the soft winter light.

Hope drifts on winds, sweet and clear,
A promise of spring when the thaw draws near.
Yet for now, we savor this icy embrace,
In the tapestry of frost, we find our place.

Hushed Cries of the Landscape

Underneath the vast, sprawling skyline,
The earth whispers softly, a subtle sign.
Mountains stand tall, their shadows loom,
In valleys below, wildflowers bloom.

The river flows, a tale of old,
Carving paths through the landscape bold.
Each ripple sings of stories untold,
In the embrace of nature, warm and cold.

Forests hum low with a calming tune,
As daylight fades and the stars commune.
Creatures stir in the cloak of night,
Hushed cries echo, a fleeting fright.

Winds carry secrets through trees so tall,
Nature's voice resounds in the quiet call.
Pebbles scatter like thoughts on the run,
In the whispers of dusk, we become one.

Upon this land, we tread soft and light,
Listening closely to nature's insight.
Every rustle, every breeze conveys,
The hushed cries of the landscape's praise.

The Still Serenade

In twilight's hush, the world stands still,
A serenade of silence, the heart to fill.
Moonlight dances on the tranquil lake,
As stars shimmer and a soft breeze wakes.

Shadows stretch long on the velvet ground,
With echoes of nature's softest sound.
Whispers of night in a fairy-tale rhyme,
In this stillness, we pause, losing track of time.

Crickets chirp their sweet lullabies,
While fireflies twinkle like distant skies.
Every breath is a note of serene,
In the still serenade, a hidden dream.

Mountains watch over with a patient grace,
Guardians of secrets, they hold in place.
In the calm of night, life feels renewed,
The whispers of nature, a soulful interlude.

Here in this moment, worries dissolve,
In the still serenade, we evolve.
With hearts entwined, let our souls dance free,
In the quiet embrace of eternity.

Crystal Echoes

In the morning light, the world ignites,
With crystal echoes, glimmering sights.
Each drop of dew, a diamond's gleam,
Nature awakens from a slumbering dream.

Mountains reflect in shimmering lakes,
Mirrors of beauty, where stillness wakes.
Birdsongs fill the air with a vibrant cheer,
In the heart of nature, we draw near.

Leaves rustle softly in the gentle breeze,
Whispers of stories in the swaying trees.
Every branch tells of seasons long flown,
In crystal echoes, our roots are sown.

Clouds sail slowly in a sky so blue,
Painting the heavens with every hue.
The sun caresses the morning skies,
In its warm embrace, nature sighs.

Life unfolds in these precious moments,
With every heartbeat, a new component.
In the symphony of earth, our spirits flow,
In the crystal echoes, together we grow.

Milton Keynes UK
Ingram Content Group UK Ltd.
UKHW010230111224
452348UK00011B/630